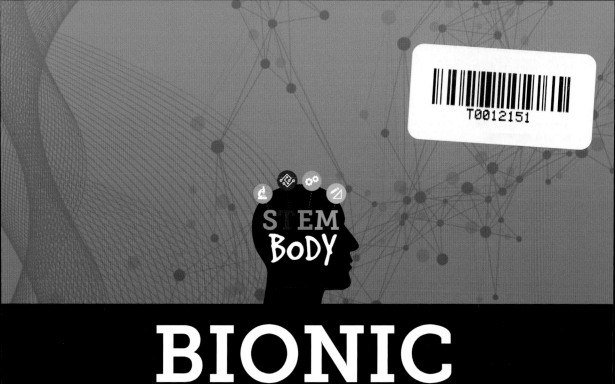

STEM
BODY

BIONIC

Bionic Bodies
STEM Body

Full Tilt Press
42964 Osgood Road
Fremont, CA 94539
readfulltilt.com

Full Tilt Press publications may be purchased for educational, business, or sales promotional use.

Editorial Credits
Design and layout by Sara Radka
Edited by Renae Gilles
Copyedited by Nikki Ramsay

Image Credits
Getty Images: Aude Guerrucci-Pool, 27 (bottom), Carlos Alvarez, 26 (bottom), E+, 4, 9
(bottom), iStockphoto, 11, 15 (top), 24, background, Mark Runnacles, 6, Tristan Fewings/
LEGO, 27 (top), 28 (bottom); Newscom: Jim Thompson/Albuquerque Journal via ZUMA Wire,
12, Kim Hairston/Baltimore Sun/MCT, 8, Kyodo, 26 (top), MCT, 22, Nikolai Galkin/TASS via
ZUMA Press, 15 (bottom), Peter Byrne/PA Wire via ZUMA Press, 18, 28 (top), Sergii Iaremenko/
Science Photo Library, 17, Visual via ZUMA Press, 14; Pixabay: louanapires, background (paper
texture); Shutterstock: CLIPAREA I Custom media, 20, Elnur, 21 (bottom), goffkein.pro, 21 (top),
kung_tom, 29; Wikimedia: Jon Bodsworth, 9 (top), Science Museum London, 9 (middle)

ISBN: 978-1-62920-836-7 (library binding)
ISBN: 978-1-62920-848-0 (ePub)

CONTENTS

INTRODUCTION

Millions of people in the United States are missing limbs. Their lives can be aided by technology.

A girl walks down the street on metal legs. They are purple, her favorite color. She enters the home of her grandparents. Their minds are as healthy as when they were young. They have brain implants that stopped brain disease. The girl's brother plays with his friends in the backyard. He searches for a hidden object with his **infrared** sight. His eye zooms in to look closer.

Sound impossible? These wonders may soon be a reality. Researchers in the STEM field of bionics are working toward goals like these. STEM stands for science, technology, engineering, and mathematics. Experts working in STEM sometimes work in bionics. Bionics combines the human body with machines. Progress is being made quickly. Understanding the **nervous system** is important to bionics. So is the tech that makes electronics really small. Combining these two things has led to incredible breakthroughs in bionics.

infrared: rays of light that cannot be seen and that have a wavelength greater than red light

nervous system: the system in a living body that directs electricity to control movement and feeling

Thought-Controlled
PROSTHETICS

In 2015, nine-year-old Josh Cathcart was fitted with a bionic hand in Scotland.

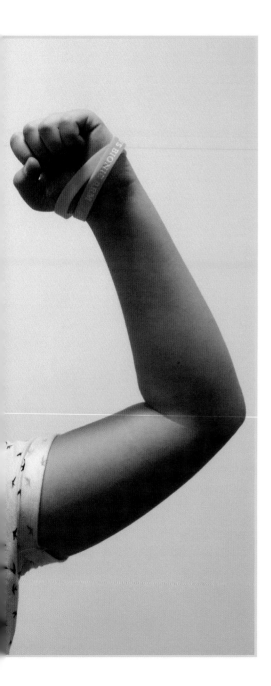

Prosthetics are artificial limbs. People get them when an arm or leg is removed. Prosthetic limbs used to have limited movement. New bionic limbs are small machines. They are connected to the user's brain. People can move them with their thoughts. These thought-controlled limbs let people move more naturally.

The human brain is complex. It has 86 billion **neurons**. It is difficult to connect a brain to a machine. But scientists are making progress. The company Ossur makes thought-controlled prosthetic feet. The University of Pittsburgh Medical Center (UPMC) has a bionics project. It helps **paralyzed** people move artificial arms with just their thoughts.

neuron: a nerve cell that carries messages throughout the body

paralyzed: when an animal or human is unable to move

The surgery to connect Ossur's bionic foot is easy. It takes 15 minutes. A small cut is made. It is only 0.4 inches (1 centimeter) long. Signals from the brain move to the base of the original leg. Tiny sensors are attached to muscles there. The sensors send signals to the bionic foot. Sensors are powered by magnetic coils. They never need batteries.

At UPMC, researchers put chips and wires in the brain. This makes a brain–machine **interface** (BMI). The BMI goes into the part of the brain that controls movement and touch. First the patient thinks about moving their arm. Then the BMI picks up this brain signal. A machine sticks out of the patient's skull. It sends the signal to the robotic arm.

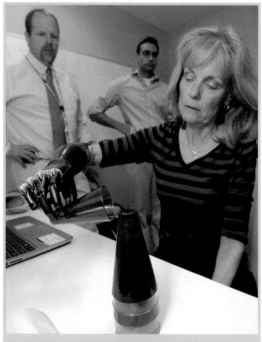

It took Anne Mekalian many hours of practice to learn to use a thought-controlled prosthetic hand.

Most of this is only possible in the **lab**. Researchers are working on limbs that can be used in everyday life. Prosthetics also need to give patients a sense of touch. When the limb touches an object, it should send the brain information on how it feels. Future STEM scientists can figure out how to do this with bionics.

---

interface: a place where different things meet and interact

lab: short for "laboratory"; a place with scientific equipment used for experiments and tests

Timeline of Prosthetics

950–710 BC The earliest-known prosthetic is a toe found on an Egyptian mummy.

300 BC Romans build the earliest-known prosthetic leg. It is made from metal and wood.

476–1000 (Middle Ages) Peg legs and hook hands are common. Knights have prosthetics that do not look like hands. Instead they are clamps that can hold a shield.

1400s–1600s (The Renaissance) Copper, iron, steel, and wood are used for prosthetics.

1863 During the US Civil War, soldiers have cosmetic rubber hands with moving fingers or attachments such as brushes.

1945 Following World War II, most prosthetic limbs are made of wood and leather.

1970s–1990s Plastics and other man-made materials are used for prosthetics. So are lightweight materials, such as **carbon fiber**.

2000–present Many new prosthetic devices are created. Athletes use lightweight running blades. Prosthetic legs and feet are specialized for rocky terrain. Motorized hands can be controlled by tiny computers.

---

carbon fiber: a very strong material made of thin pieces of carbon

BIONIC LIMB

Thought-controlled bionic limbs are made by teams of people. They are all in STEM fields such as medicine, computer engineering, and materials science.

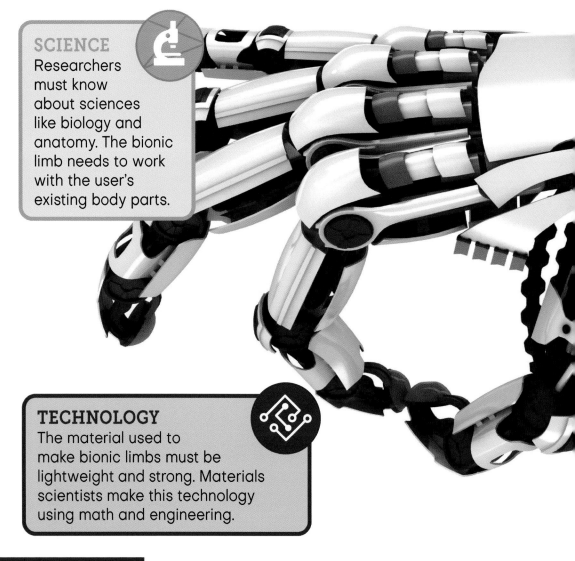

SCIENCE
Researchers must know about sciences like biology and anatomy. The bionic limb needs to work with the user's existing body parts.

TECHNOLOGY
The material used to make bionic limbs must be lightweight and strong. Materials scientists make this technology using math and engineering.

ENGINEERING

The limb's chips and processors read and translate signals from the body. Computer engineers design the software and hardware. Math is important to this field too.

MATH

New bionic limbs can predict a person's movement, then respond quickly. Scientists program the limbs using math problems called algorithms. Algorithms make the predictions used by the bionic limbs.

Bionic ORGANS

The HeartMate II is an LVAD. It is 3 inches (8 cm) long and weighs 10 ounces (300 grams). That's about as big as a can of soup.

More than 100,000 Americans are on organ **transplant** waiting lists. Patients sometimes die before they get one. Even after they get a new organ, their body might reject it. This means the body fights against the new organ.

Machines can help damaged organs work better. The LVAD is one of these. It stands for "left ventricular assist device." This helps the heart pump blood. It uses batteries. Scientists are working on a **titanium** heart too.

One problem with machines is that the body grows scars around them. Bionic organs can avoid that kind of rejection. They can be made with bioprinting. This is a kind of **3-D printing**. Special printers lay down layers. Some layers are human cells. Others are man-made materials. Together they form bionic flesh. An organ could be bioprinted from a patient's own cells. Then their body would be less likely to reject it.

transplant: an operation in which an organ or body part is removed from one person and put into the body of another person

titanium: a very strong, lightweight metal

3-D printing: a process where a three-dimensional object is created from a computer model by adding material one layer at a time

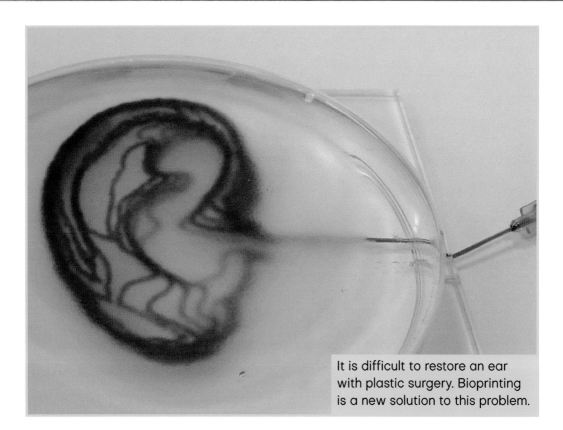

It is difficult to restore an ear with plastic surgery. Bioprinting is a new solution to this problem.

Princeton University researchers have bioprinted a bionic ear. The scientists used a 3-D printer they bought online. They printed an ear from cow cells and hydrogel. Hydrogel is a special gel. Live cells are mixed in. The gel dissolves once the printing is done, leaving just the cells.

Silver **nanoparticles** are also a part of the bionic ear. They were used to print an antenna inside it. The bionic ear can hear much better than normal human ears. It can pick up radio waves that usually only a radio can hear. This ear is not yet ready to be used by humans.

---

nanoparticle: a particle between 1 and 100 nanometers in size (1 to 100 millionth of a millimeter)

Bionic Pancreas

Almost 10 percent of Americans have diabetes. This is a disease where an organ called the pancreas does not work correctly. It cannot control how much sugar is in the blood. Diabetics test their blood every day. They take medicine. A man-made pancreas is being designed in England. It uses a gel that contains medicine. The gel dissolves when there is too much sugar in the blood. This releases medicine. Then the gel hardens again until more medicine is needed.

In Russia, scientists printed a bionic thyroid gland. It was for a mouse. The thyroid is a small organ in the neck. It delivers important chemicals called hormones. When scientists can make human thyroids, many diseases could be treated. With further advances in STEM fields, any organ a human needs could be printed.

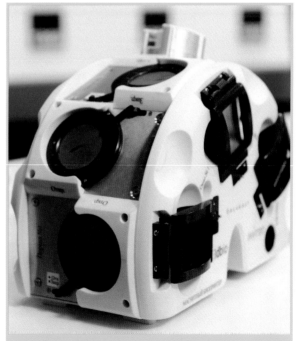

The Organaut 3-D printer is part of a bioprinting experiment on the International Space Station.

BIOPRINTER

Bioprinting uses a 3-D printer to build human body parts such as organs. People from several STEM fields contribute to this complex technology.

SCIENCE

A deep knowledge of biology and medicine is necessary to correctly design printed organs. Computer science is required since designs are made on computers.

TECHNOLOGY

The machine used to print the organs is often a 3-D printer. This technology began in the 1980s as a way to quickly make parts for machines.

ENGINEERING

The hydrogel and nanoparticles used to print organs are created by tissue engineers. They need to know about both engineering and biology.

MATH

To create a bioprinted organ, many math calculations must be solved. Scientists calculate the exact dimensions of the organ. Then they program the 3-D printer.

3D printer

Bionic EYES

Raymond Flynn received an Argus II bionic eye in 2015. He was the first person to see with natural and artificial vision at the same time.

Prosthetic eyes have been used for centuries. They replace an eyeball that has been removed. These eyes do not see. Bionic eyes are new. They give sight to an eyeball that is blind. The **US Food and Drug Administration** (FDA) approved the first bionic eye in 2013. It is called the Argus II.

The Argus II is for patients with an eye disease. It is called retinitis pigmentosa (RP). RP affects more than 2 million people worldwide. With the Argus II, people can see in black and white. They can see the outline of a doorway, the movement of a person, or the lines on a crosswalk. Some have even been able to read large letters.

US Food and Drug Administration: a federal agency responsible for protecting public health in the United States

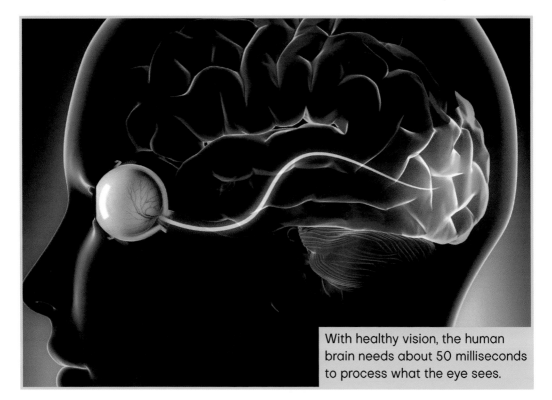

With healthy vision, the human brain needs about 50 milliseconds to process what the eye sees.

For normal vision, light first hits the **retina**. It turns the light into signals. The **optic nerve** sends the signals to the brain. In many kinds of blindness, the retina or optic nerve is damaged. Bionic eyes help bridge the gap between light and the brain. These bionics use eyeglasses and eye implants.

With the Argus II, patients wear a pair of glasses with a camera. The camera records visual information. A small computer unit reads the information. The unit sends a signal to 60 wires attached to the patient's eyeball. The wires then send a signal to the optic nerve. This transfers messages to the brain.

retina: light-sensitive tissues at the back of the eyeball

optic nerve: a bundle of nerve fibers at the back of the eye that carries visual messages to the brain

Super Eyes

A company called Ocumetics is testing a bionic lens. It replaces the eyeball's natural lens. It would give perfect eyesight. Distance vision would be completely clear. The company wants to add other features next. One is a smartphone screen displayed to the eye.

Other researchers have made contact lenses with tiny telescopes. They can zoom in and out. They cannot be worn for long. This is because they stop air from reaching the eyeball.

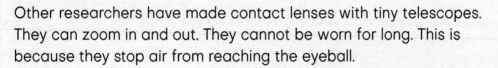

In the future, the Argus II will have more wires. This will make for sharper vision. Color vision may even be possible. Researchers are also making a bionic eye that sends information from glasses directly into the brain. This will help when an eyeball is damaged or missing. More work in STEM is needed to get these new bionic eyes working.

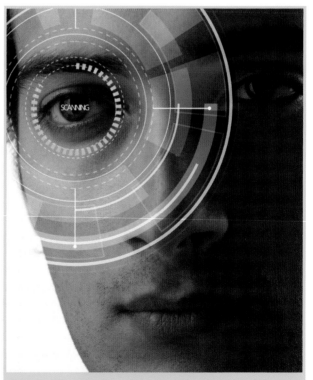

Nearly 40 million people around the world are blind. More than 1 billion suffer from poor vision. Bionics can help restore sight to many of these people.

BIONIC EYEBALL

STEM researchers are behind the theory and technology of bionic eyes. Cameras record light. Microchips and wires change light into electrical signals. The signals then enter the brain.

SCIENCE

In order to replace the function of the eye, ophthalmologists had to first understand it. Neuroscientists had to learn how it connected to the brain.

TECHNOLOGY
Scientists must design eye implants with materials safe to use inside the body. Physics helps them understand the interactions.

EYE IMPLANT

EYE

ENGINEERING
Computer engineers are part of the varied team that helps create bionic eyes. They are part of creating and programming the microchips that receive the camera signals.

MATH
Biomedical engineers build medical devices. They use math to calculate things like the fit of the device in the body.

The Bionic Bodies
COMMUNITY

Students interested in bionics should see if there is a robotics club to join. They can also study STEM subjects, such as biology, physics, and engineering.

Everyone behind bionics works in STEM. Bionics is a science that uses technology. The technology requires engineering. A strong foundation in math is also needed for this work.

STEM workers started learning their skills in middle and high school. They took chemistry and biology classes. They might have been in robotics clubs. Many of them now work in universities. Researchers from different fields work together. Companies also make bionics. The US government **invests** in the field. The military would like to use bionic body parts for soldiers.

Bionic technology is moving forward by leaps and bounds. It helps many people live more comfortably. This is thanks to the many scientists, engineers, and doctors working on bionics.

invest: to spend money in order to help something or make something better

BIONICS SCIENTISTS

STEM workers from around the world are leading the way in bionics science.

CYBERDYNE

Cyberdyne made an **exoskeleton** for paralyzed people. It is thought-controlled. The suit touches the user's skin. When brain signals reach the skin, the suit moves in response. Then the patient's brain gets a message that the body has moved. This helps patients learn to move on their own.

HUGH HERR

Hugh Herr is a physicist and engineer. At 17, he was caught in a blizzard for three days. His legs had to be removed below the knees. His prosthetic legs couldn't climb. So Herr designed a different pair of legs. Then he went back to climbing. He also went to school for STEM.

---

exoskeleton: a hard covering for the body that provides support or protection

biophysicist: a scientist who uses physics to study biology

DAVID AGUILAR

This teenager from Spain is a **bioengineering** student. He was born without a right forearm. Aguilar built himself an arm. It was made of LEGOs. At 18, he built a working robotic arm. It bent at the elbow and could pick things up. He is already using his fourth model. The young man's dream is to design affordable robotic limbs for those who need them.

EASTON LaCHAPPELLE

Easton LaChappelle brought a robotic arm to his eighth-grade science fair. That day, he met a little girl. Her basic prosthetic arm had cost her family more than $80,000. LaChappelle decided he would build an affordable robotic prosthetic. As an adult, he runs the company Unlimited Tomorrow. It makes artificial limbs at the lowest cost possible.

bioengineering: the use of artificial tissue to replace damaged parts of the body, such as artificial limbs

QUIZ

1 What does STEM stand for?

2 How many neurons are in the human brain?

3 What is the earliest-known prosthetic?

4 What are the two types of layers in bioprinting?

5 What is the FDA-approved bionic eyeball called?

6 What do biomedical engineers do?

7 What did David Aguilar first use to make an arm?

8 What does Easton LaChappelle's company, Unlimited Tomorrow, do?

ACTIVITY

Argumentative Essay

Bionics are advanced pieces of technology. They can heal people and extend their lifetimes. They can give people enhanced abilities. But bionics can also be expensive. Only certain people might be able to afford them.

Social inequality is when only some people receive certain benefits. They are usually more wealthy than others. Consider this statement: "Bionics will lead to social inequality." Conduct research and write an argumentative essay on this statement.

STEPS

1. Use your favorite search engine, or ask your favorite librarian, to find out more about bionics and equality. Here are some questions you might want to answer: How expensive are bionics? How many people currently have access?

2. Think about your findings. Form your opinion on the statement "Bionics will lead to social inequality."

3. Write an outline. Your essay should state your opinion clearly up front. It should explain the reasons why you are correct. Try coming up with three unique reasons. Organize the paper by including one reason per paragraph.

4. Write the essay. Have a classmate read it and give suggestions for changes.

5. Take it further: Set up a debate on the topic. Use your essay to inform your side.

GLOSSARY

3-D printing: a process where a three-dimensional object is created from a computer model by adding material one layer at a time

bioengineering: the use of artificial tissue to replace damaged parts of the body, such as artificial limbs

biophysicist: a scientist who uses physics to study biology

carbon fiber: a very strong material made of thin pieces of carbon

exoskeleton: a hard covering for the body that provides support or protection

infrared: rays of light that cannot be seen and that have a wavelength greater than red light

interface: a place where different things meet and interact

invest: to spend money in order to help something or make something better

lab: short for "laboratory"; a place with scientific equipment used for experiments and tests

nanoparticle: a particle between 1 and 100 nanometers in size (1 to 100 millionth of a millimeter)

nervous system: the system in a living body that directs electricity to control movement and feeling

neuron: a nerve cell that carries messages throughout the body

optic nerve: a bundle of nerve fibers at the back of the eye that carries visual messages to the brain

paralyzed: when an animal or human is unable to move

retina: light-sensitive tissues at the back of the eyeball

titanium: a very strong, lightweight metal

transplant: an operation in which an organ or body part is removed from one person and put into the body of another person

US Food and Drug Administration: a federal agency responsible for protecting public health in the United States

READ MORE

Arnold, Nick. *Tools, Robotics, and Gadgets Galore.* STEM Quest. Hauppauge, NY: Barrons Educational Series, Inc., 2018.

Bethea, Nikole Brooks. *Discover Bionics.* What's Cool about Science? Minneapolis: Lerner Publications, 2017.

Furstinger, Nancy. *Unstoppable: True Stories of Amazing Bionic Animals.* Boston: Houghton Mifflin Harcourt, 2017.

Marquardt, Meg. *How Do Bionic Limbs Work?* How Do They Do That? North Mankato, MN: Capstone Press, 2019.

Small, Cathleen. *Diversity in Medicine.* Diversity in Action. New York: Rosen Central, 2019.

INTERNET SITES

https://www.cdc.gov/ncbddd/kids/vision.html
Learn more about vision impairment with Kids' Quest.

https://limbitless-solutions.org/OBF
Watch video stories of kids whose lives have been changed by bionic limbs.

https://kids.britannica.com/students/article/bionics/273221
Visit Britannica Kids for more information on bionics.

https://science.howstuffworks.com/prosthetic-limb1.htm
Read more about the history of prosthetics.

http://www.kidsciencechallenge.com/#/home
Check out the Kids' Science Challenge for games, videos, and info on STEM careers.

INDEX